OUR JOURNEY OF LENT

Rev. J. Ronald Knott

Sophronismos Press
Louisville, Kentucky

Our Journey of Lent

For information address:
Sophronismos Press
1271 Parkway Gardens Court #106
Louisville, Kentucky 40217

Cover Design & Book Layout: Tim Schoenbachler

First Printing: January 21, 2018

ISBN: 978-0-9962445-5-8

Also by J. Ronald Knott

All books published by Sophronismos Press

BOOKS FOR CLERGY

Intentional Presbyterates
(Spanish and Swahili editions available)

From Seminarian to Diocesan Priest
(Spanish edition available)

The Spiritual Leadership of a Parish Priest
(Spanish & Vietnamese editions available)

Intentional Presbyterates: The Workbook

A Bishop and His Priests Together

The Character of a Pastor in Exercising Authority

Personal Growth Plan: A Handbook for Priests

HOMILIES / SPIRITUALITY

An Encouraging Word: *Renewed Hearts, Renewed Church*

One Heart at a Time: *Renewing the Church in the New Millennium*

Sunday Nights: *Encouraging Words for Young Adults*

Affirming Goodness

The Lord Is Close to the Brokenhearted

A Passion for Personal and Vocational Excellence

FOR THE RECORD BOOK SERIES

FOR THE RECORD:
Encouraging Words for Ordinary Catholics, Volumes I - XV

For information about eBook and printed editions of Father Knott's books, go to: www.ronknottbooks.com

DEDICATION

To Gary and Rita Marvin,
a source of
ongoing encouragement
over the years.

ACKNOWLEDGMENTS

I would like to thank, in a very special way, Mr. Tim Schoenbachler, who formatted this book and many of my books into e-books and new print editions as well as created and maintains my website where all my books are available in one convenient place. He has offered me so much wise advice and counsel over the years and made it possible for me to share my work with even more people.

Last of all, I would like to thank the many supportive people who have attended my Parish Missions and who have encouraged me to keep on preaching and writing and who have taken the time to let me know how much these words of encouragement have meant to them.

TABLE OF CONTENTS

Preface

Wouldn't Take Nothing for My Journey Now

"Every person needs to take one day away. A day in which one consciously separates the past from the future. Jobs, lovers, family, employers, and friends can exist one day without any one of us, and if our egos permit us to confess, they could exist eternally in our absence. Each person deserves a day away in which no problems are confronted, no solutions searched for. Each of us needs to withdraw from the cares which will not withdraw from us. We need hours of aimless wandering or spates of time sitting on park benches, observing the mysterious world of ants and the canopy of treetops. If we step away for a time, we are not, as many may think and some will accuse, being irresponsible, but rather we are preparing ourselves to more ably perform our duties and discharge our obligations. When I return home, I am always surprised to find some questions I sought to evade had been answered and some entanglements I had hoped to flee had become unraveled in my absence. A day away acts as a spring tonic. It can dispel rancor, transform indecision, and renew the spirit."

– MAYA ANGELOU

THE WHOLE POINT OF LENT

Return to me with your whole heart, says the Lord.
Joel 2:12

When I was a kid growing up in Meade County, I used to come to Louisville with my Dad a few times a week to pick up supplies for his building material business. We always took Dixie Highway, the mother of all road sign highways – at least back then! After hundreds of trips and millions of signs, the *only* one I can remember today, fifty years later, is a huge sign around Waverly Hills. In huge letters, it demanded that its readers "Get right with God!"

"Get right with God!" That is pretty much what this season of Lent is all about. It is a sacred forty-day journey when we get back on our spiritual paths by reconsidering how far we have strayed from that path and make a u-turn. It's a time to "get right with God."

THE DISCIPLINES OF LENT

Jesus told us that we are to "love God with our whole hearts, souls and minds and our neighbor as ourselves." That is the gold standard, the starting point and the measure of our faith. And so, during Lent, we break that one commandment down and focus on its three components. We focus on **prayer** – nourishing our relationship with God. We focus on **fasting** – our relationship to our own appetites. We focus on **giving alms** – our care and love for others, especially on our suffering poor brothers and sisters. So Lent, really, is about getting back to basics and "making the important things important again."

At the very beginning of this holy season, in the gospel for Ash Wednesday, Jesus warns us not to act like "actors in a play" with our silly little mind games.

(1) "**When you pray,**" he says, "don't draw attention to yourself as a cheap attempt at impressing others. Do it quietly. Make it something between you and God." In other words, if you resolve to pray more during this holy season, don't announce it to everyone in the house and neighborhood that you are going to go to say the rosary every day, don't make a public announcement that you

are going to Mass in the morning because "it is my Lenten resolution." No! Keep it between yourself and God. Just slip away quietly. Try not to let anyone know about it.

(2) "**When you fast**," Jesus says, "don't wear it on your sleeve for everyone to know about! Do it quietly. Make it something between you and God." In other words, if you resolve to give up beer or chocolate, don't tell anybody about it. Don't go wringing your hands complaining bitterly about how you are suffering from this tragic loss in your life and how heroic you are for doing it. When you skip a meal or turn down a trip to have beer, try not to let *anybody* know why. And by the way, the money you save by doing this is not to be *kept*, but *given away*. Neither is fasting about losing a few pounds for spring break!

(3) "**When you give alms**," Jesus says, "don't make a public announcement about your gift or brag about how generous you are." Make anonymous contributions to food pantries, charitable organizations, alternative spring break programs or your parish social service committee. Don't even write a check to use as a tax deduction or ask for a plaque to be dedicated in your honor. Try to be as anonymous as possible. Make it a pure gift.

The entire gospel for Ash Wednesday is not only about doing good things, but even more so about doing them for the right reason. We do not pray, fast and give alms to gain sympathy or praise from others. We do not pray or give alms to be noticed and admired. We do not fast to save money or to lose weight. We fast for two major reasons. We fast so that we can experience how much eating we do for all the wrong reasons. We fast so that we will have more to share with the hungry when we give alms.

In short, our **external** Lenten practices only have value if they trigger an **internal shift**. It's about "getting right with God, ourselves and our neighbors." It is better *not* to go up and receive ashes if you are not committed to "getting right with God" in a quiet, private, you-and-God kind of way. God can see right through your hypocrisy and fake religiosity. Don't waste your time playing games with God and those around you. The goal here is a serious internal change, getting you heart "right with God."

So that this internal shift may happen, we use these traditional spiritual disciplines while we are on a journey. On this spiritual internal journey, we go to some very specific places where we might have a chance to encounter God, places where we can be changed internally by that encounter. These stops on the journey are spiritual places, not geographic places that can be seen on a map. We are invited to go to symbolic deserts, mountains, wells, doctors and cemeteries so as to be changed while we are there.

Places Where We Go to Encounter God in Lent

First, We are Invited to the Desert

The Spirit drove Jesus out into the desert where he remained for forty days.

Mark 1:12

On Ash Wednesday, we opened the holy season of Lent, receiving ashes as an outward sign of our willingness to get serious about conversion of life, about "getting right with God," as the Dixie Highway sign read. The rector of the seminary where I used to work is a convert from the Baptist Church. He is intensely attracted to the traditional signs and symbols of the Catholic Church. As a result, he tends to get carried away sometimes. Those who received ashes from life-long Catholics like me got a modest cross in the center of their foreheads. Those who got in his line got a cross that went from hairlines-to-the-top-of-the-nose and from ear-to-ear! They stood out in the cafeteria after Mass because they looked like they had been hit by a coal truck! They were the laughing stock of the lunch line!

Using our Sunday readings for the five weeks of Lent, I would like to make the case that conversion of life requires that we go to the desert, go to the mountain, go to the well, go to the doctor and go to the grave to get the insights we need to be created anew.

On the first Sunday of Lent, to be created anew during these days of Lent, Jesus invites us to go to the desert, an empty place where there is nothing to distract, a symbolic place of laser-focused attention.

If we are to be serious about conversion of life, we must first be willing to withdraw from the noise and pace of ordinary life, at least for a little a while, so that we can hear ourselves think and receive direction from the Spirit. As the ancient Chinese proverb puts it, "Outside noisy, inside empty!" In other words, you cannot "get right with God" unless you put yourself somewhere where you can hear his whispering voice. **God doesn't shout, he whispers!**

Most of us cannot afford forty days of "retreat," heading off to some monastery or even to a secluded cabin in the woods. We must "make do" with an hour here, an afternoon there or, if we are lucky, a whole day.

In preparing to write my lenten presentation, I read a few articles about multitasking. What they seemed to agree on is this: we all have an ever-present pressure of trying to cram more and more into each moment. We are inundated with faster and faster gadgets to do more and more in a shorter amount of time. Ironically, all the articles I read seemed to agree. The more we use such gadgets and the more we try to handle at one time, the more inefficient our brains become.

Multitasking is an illusion. There is evidence that our brains cannot concentrate on more than one complex task at a time. The more information our brains are forced to handle simultaneously, the more they slow down. Tasks take longer. Mistakes multiply. Real efficiency is found in mono-tasking, not multitasking. For this very reason, more states have prohibited talking on cell phones and texting while driving.

What is even scarier is the theory that bombarding our brains with bursts of information is undermining our ability to focus. These bursts of information play into a primitive impulse to respond to immediate opportunities and threats. This stimulation provokes excitement – a dopamine squirt – that researchers say can be addictive. In its absence, people feel bored. I know at least two younger priests whom I consider to be addicted to technology gadgets.

I noticed an advertisement on TV the other day that captures the spirit of "going to the desert." I am sure some of you have seen it. Chevy Trucks has a commercial with "the guys" going deeper and deeper into the woods until they finally get a "no signal" on their cell phones! With that, they let out a yelp of delight! Maybe one of the best things many people can do during this season, and probably a very hard thing to do, is to go somewhere for an hour or two where your electronic gadgets are turned off or somewhere where you can get "no signal" and just "be!" I guarantee you that it will be harder than you think! For some of you, one hour without being technologically connected will be as hard as trying to go without oxygen. But that's the point of all the disciplines of Lent – **to find out who and what controls our lives.** Is it overeating, overdrinking, over drugging, overscheduling or even over-texting or over-posting? When we "give it up for Lent" we find out how much power it has over us and how little power we have over it! That is the real point of "giving things up for Lent" – to test who is really in control here. The idea is to enlighten ourselves about ourselves, not simply pointlessly punishing ourselves. God is more interested in us knowing ourselves than us punishing ourselves.

In Lent we go to the desert, so to speak, in order to re-learn how to be fully present to ourselves, to each other and to God! Are you brave enough to face your relationship with yourself, your relationships with others and your relationship with God? If you are, then "do Lent" the way it is meant to be done - seriously, with thought and with spiritual maturity!

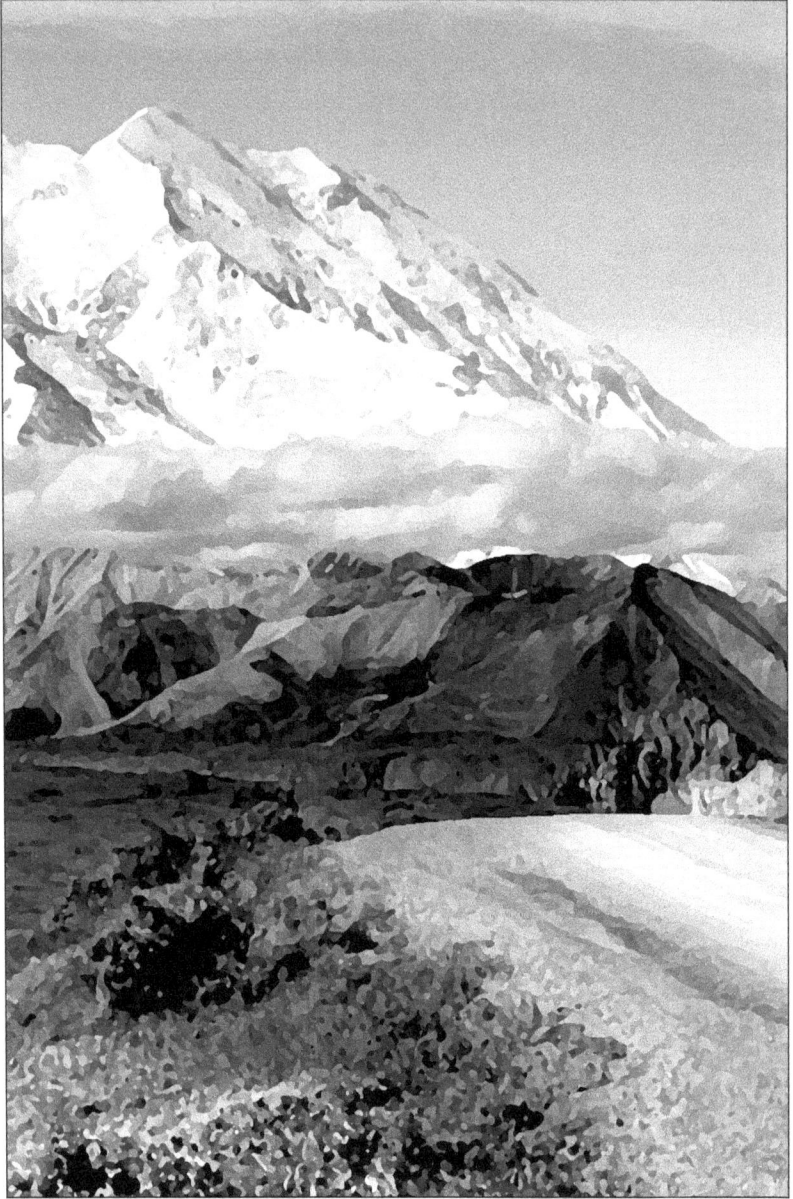

SECOND, WE ARE INVITED
TO THE MOUNTAIN

Jesus took Peter, James and John and
led them up a high mountain apart by themselves.
Mark 9:2

After being invited the first week of Lent to "go to the desert" for new insights into ourselves, we are invited the second week of Lent to "go to the mountain" for a **new perspective.**

When Jesus came out of the desert, the first thing he called for was a radical new outlook – *metanoia!* On the second Sunday of Lent, Jesus invites us to go to the mountaintop, a traditional place for achieving a new perspective on life. From a mountaintop you can see in all directions. Jesus invites us to go the mountaintop because conversion of life, the real purpose of Lent, is impossible without a change of perspective, without a new way of seeing.

It is easy to "get stuck" in the way we think. As Brooks Atkinson put it, "The most fatal illusion is the settled point of view." Some of us go through life living out the old joke, "Don't confuse me with the facts, my mind is made up!" Even scientists have trouble incorporating new information. The French Academy announced at one point that it would not accept any further reports of meteorites, since it was clearly impossible for rocks to fall out of the sky. Shortly thereafter a rain of meteorites came close to breaking the windows of the Academy. Lent is a time to take a long, loving look at reality.

Dr. Wayne Dyer teaches us that, "When you change the way you look at things, the things you look at change." This is certainly true in resolving soul-eating anger and resentment toward other people. What many people fail to realize is that there is a "way out" when offending people refuse to apologize and own the hurt they have caused. What they fail to realize is that the hurt can be healed and the problem resolved with a new way of looking at the perpetrator. Lent is a time to change the way we look at others.

John Lubbock reminds us that "What we see depends mainly on what we look for!" Oscar Wilde put it humorously when he said, "The optimist sees the donut; the pessimist sees the hole." The more attention you shine on a particular subject, the more evidence of it will grow. Shine attention on obstacles or possibilities and they will multiply lavishly. Lent is a time to change the way we look at the world.

Possibly the most important change we need to make this Lent in our perspective is the way we view ourselves.

No one has said it better than Marianne Williamson. "Our deepest fear is not that we are inadequate; our deepest fear is that we are powerful beyond measure. It is our light, not our darkness, that most frightens us. We were born to make manifest the glory of God within us. It is not just in some of us; it is in everyone, and as we let our own light shine, we unconsciously give other people permission to do the same." Lent is a time to get a new perspective. Lent is a time to see the world through God's eyes.

Because of the "transfiguration" gospel, they are called "peak experiences" – those intense religious experiences that many of us have been lucky enough to have at least once in our lives. In fact, I believe that this is the main thing that keeps people in organized religion - at least one "peak experience." On the other hand, it is also the main reason some people claim to be agnostic - the absence of even one "peak experience."

"Peak experiences" cannot be staged or created. They are simply moments of grace – spontaneous gifts from God. We can go to places where "peak experiences" have happened to other people, even places where we have personally experienced them before, but that does not mean we will have another one. They are simply unpredictable and unannounced gifts from God.

"Peak experiences" can happen at some of the most surprising times and in some of the most unlikely places. Oddly enough, for example, during the sexual abuse storm that began in 2002 a significant number of journalists, who had been assigned to report on the crisis in various locales, ended up converting to Catholicism. They had a "religious experience," a "peak experience" even in the midst of that pain and sin! Others have had these "peak experiences" during the death process of a loved one or even their own process of dying. I witnessed my mother going through one of these "peak experiences" as she was dying of cancer back in 1976.

"Peak experiences" happen most often during retreats and other religious events. For instance, many seminarians were so moved by meeting Pope John Paul II that they came back to the Church, after having been gone since childhood, and even decided that they may have a call to the priesthood. Many teenagers have their first "peak experience" during their senior retreat or an alternative spring break in places like Guatemala. Many married couples have had life changing "peak experiences" during Marriage Encounter weekends. Other Catholics have discovered a new burst of faith during a Cursillo weekend, a trip to Medjugore or Lourdes, even meeting someone with the stature of Mother Teresa.

How they happen, why they happen and when they happen cannot be predicted, staged or even understood. They all seem to be glimpses into another level of existence or little previews of coming wonderful events that God gives some people who need a reason to hang on! Those of us who have experienced them know how mind-blowing and life changing they can be! To those who cannot say they have ever had such an experience, I would say "it ain't over till it's over" and "your time may be right around the corner" at some unexpected and unpredictable time.

These "peak experiences" have several things in common. You have to be open to them. The "transfiguration" that we read about today, happened during one of hundreds of little retreats that Jesus arranged for his disciples! Regular contact with God through prayer does not guarantee one of these experiences, but makes them more likely to happen. Your mind must to be open and you must remain in a receiving frame of mind.

There is always a temptation to want to freeze the experience, repeat the experience and make the experience permanent. This is what Peter was up to in the reading today. "Lord, it is so wonderful to be here. Why don't we erect some tents and just stay up here forever?" Jesus tells Peter that the experience was only meant to be something to sustain the group during the painful days ahead. He tells Peter that they will have to go back down the mountain and back into real life for a while. Experiencing it "all the time" would have to wait until the resurrection after his death. One of the things that Cursillo, Marriage Encounter, Medjugore, senior retreat,

Lourdes and other similar experiences have it common is the desire that many have to repeat those experiences or to "be in them" full time. They are never meant to be permanent. They are only glimpses into glory. God wants us to go back to our ordinary lives, with that precious moment in the back of our minds to sustain us.

Lastly, "peak experiences" are meant to help is "see connections" to see the connection between where we come from, where we are now and where we are destined. This is what the conversation that Jesus had with the saints - Moses and Elijah. This conversation helped Jesus realize that he was the one they saw coming in the future so many years before. They helped Jesus understand where God was taking him in the days ahead – glory on the other side of suffering and death. Just so, our "peak experiences" remind us that there is something wonderful in the invisible world that awaits us on the other side of this life.

May you experience your own "peak experience!" May God give you a "glimpse of glory." May you get a "sneak preview" of the world to come! May that "peak experience" sustain you in the sometimes tediousness of worldly existence and help you keep your eye on the prize.

With all the problems going on in the Church today, others ask me and I ask myself over and over again "Why stay?" The reason I stay is that I have been blessed to have had several "peak experiences" and "glimpses of glory" in my life time. It is these intense experiences that sustain me during the ordinary moments, periods of spiritual dryness and intense discouragement. As I think about all the scandal that has beset the Church, I am not worried or overcome with discouragement. To paraphrase Dr. Martin Luther King, who built his famous speech around this gospel, "I don't know what will happen now. We've got some difficult days ahead, but it doesn't matter with me now because I have been to the mountaintop. God has allowed me to go up to the mountain and I've looked over and I have seen the promised land. Mine eyes have seen the glory of the coming of the Lord!"

I am here to stay, I remain hopeful and I am committed to being faithful to the end, not because I am out of touch with the serious problems facing our Church, but because God has given me a couple of small glimpses of glory, like he did the disciples in today's gospel. I hold on because of those "peak experiences."

THIRD, WE ARE INVITED TO THE WELL

Whoever drinks the water I shall give will never thirst.
John 4:14

On the first Sunday of Lent, Jesus invited us to conversion of life by going to the desert. The desert is a place devoid of distractions, a place to gain insight. On the second Sunday of Lent, Jesus invited us to go up the mountain with him. Mountains are places where you can go to gain perspective, to get the big picture. From a mountaintop you can see into the distance – where you've been and where you are headed. On the third Sunday of Lent, Jesus invites us to go to the well, a place one goes to quench one's thirst.

In many ways, people today are thirsty, restless and looking for meaning. The prophet Haggai, about 520 years before Christ, described our culture quite well when he wrote, "You have sown much, but have brought in little; you have eaten, but have not been satisfied; you have drunk, but not been exhilarated; have clothed yourselves, but not been warmed; and you have earned wages for a bag with holes in it." We "have it all" one hand and yet we are still not satisfied on the other. We are "cravers for more!"

It has been suggested that our consumer culture has spawned a new climate of thirstiness and restlessness. The experts call it "churn," using the word to describe our short attention span and our "what's next" attitude. This restlessness is seen in a consuming lust for endless distractions and amusements. This restlessness is being fed, some believe, by the overstimulation and excessive exposure to violent movies, fast-paced videos, computers and cell-phones, loud hard-wired music and over-scheduling. All these together exacerbate agitation, restlessness and hyperactivity.

What the world seems to be craving right now is what Jesus called "rest for one's soul." He said on one occasion, "Come to me, all who labor and are heavy laden, and I will give you rest. Take my yoke upon you and learn from me, for I am gentle and lowly in heart, and you will find rest for your souls." Jesus offers "rest" to those who are "worn out" in their search for "meaning."

In this gospel, we meet a wonderful woman who is an example of all that. Jesus meets this woman at a well. She is tired - tired to the bone. She is **physically** tired - tired of being thirsty and having to constantly draw water and carry it long distances. She lived a half mile away and the well was over 100 feet deep. She was **emotionally** tired - tired of trying to find satisfying relationships in her life. She had been "looking for love in all the wrong places," as the country song goes. She had been married five times. She was tired of being discriminated against by others. Jews hated Samaritans like her and women in general were considered socially inferior. She was **spiritually** tired – tired of a burdensome religion that was not really satisfying. At the well, she meets Jesus and pours out her heart to him and he, in turn, gives her "living water" and "rest for her soul."

All of us are like this woman in some degree. We all have a void in our lives that we try to fill. Some of us strive frantically our whole lives to fill that void by gaining material things, gaining stature, gaining status, gaining fame, finding the perfect relationship and much more. The fact of the matter is we will never fill that void with "things or stuff" because that void was put there for a specific purpose. We have a built-in missing piece – given to us by God himself.

What is the purpose of that void? What is that missing piece? It is the place where God belongs. Only God can fill that hole. Saint Augustine of Hippo described it best when he said, "You have made us for yourself, O Lord, and our hearts are restless until they rest in you."

It's as if we are running around with a hole in our souls that we are desperately trying to fill. The truth of the matter is that only God can fill it, and yet we try our best to fill it with unsatisfying distractions and amusements, objects and things. Lent is a time to stop by the "well" for "living waters" and find "rest" in God.

The best meditation for this gospel could be Francis Thompson's *The Hound of Heaven*:

> I fled Him, down the nights and down the days;
> I fled Him, down the arches of the years;
> I fled Him, down the labyrinthine ways of my
>   own mind;
> and in the midst of tears I hid from Him…

I have always loved the words of Celie in the movie "The Color Purple." Celie feels a hole in her life. She is more than a bit aggravated by the feeling of God's absence in her life – what she refers to as God "just sitting up there glorifying in being deaf." She speaks for many people today when she says, "It ain't easy trying to do without God. Even if you know he ain't there trying to do without him is a strain." Those who experience the strain of trying to "do without God" will no doubt feel a hole in their souls, a hunger and thirst that nothing seems to satisfy. Lent is time to re-connect with God after "trying to do without him."

Jesus has taken us to the desert, to the mountain and to the well so that he might lead us to conversion of life, a life that is full and satisfying.

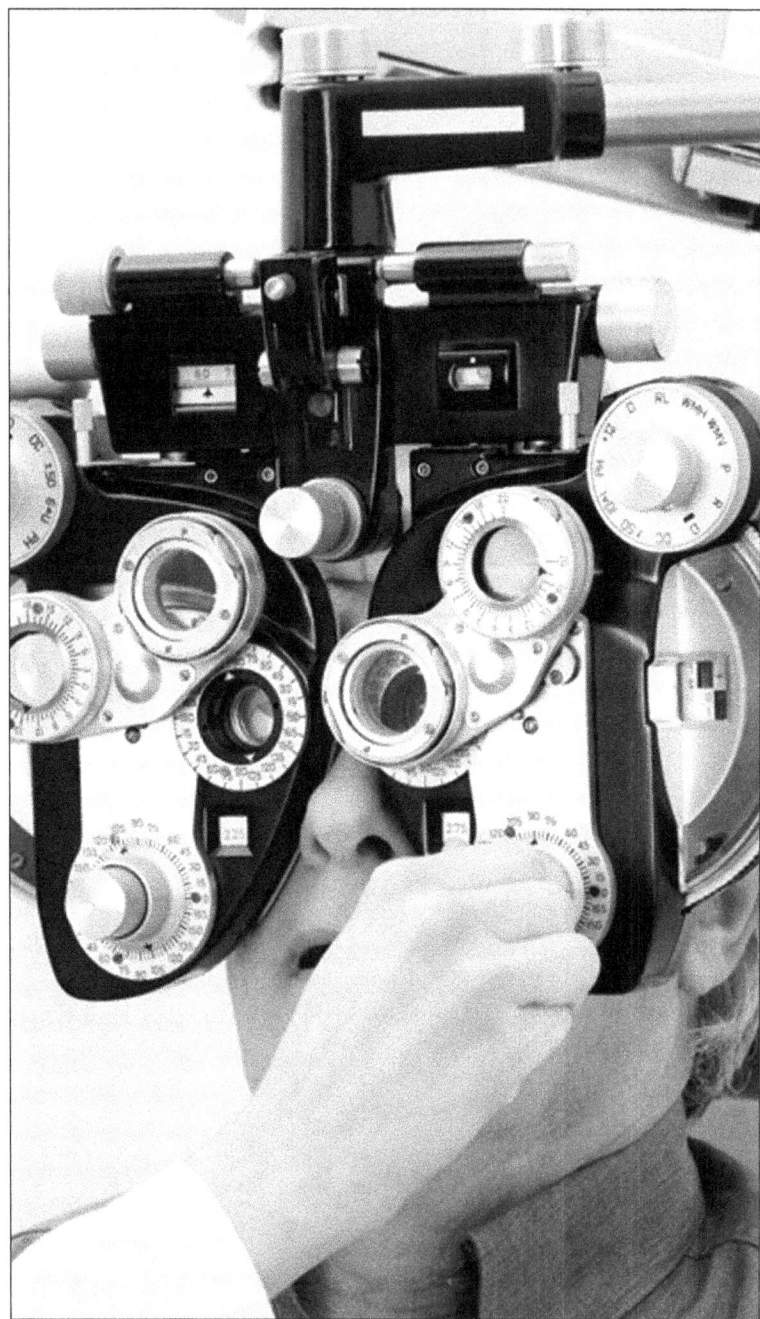

FOURTH, WE ARE INVITED TO THE DOCTOR

If you were blind, that would not be a sin. But since you say you can see, when you are actually blind, you remain in your sin.
JOHN 9:41

So far, we have been to the desert, the mountain and the well. Next, Jesus invites us to admit that we are sick and invite us to go to the doctor for healing.

Tyler Perry is a successful African-American playwright, actor and screenwriter. Perry attributes his success to what he calls "spiritual progress," especially the "spiritual progress" that resulted in making peace with his own father. One of his profound insights was around learning that "parents do what they know how." He finally realized that he could not change his history with his father, but he could change the way he wanted to remember it. "My life changed," he said, "once things changed in me."

I, too, had to learn how resentment can keep you stuck and how you can free yourself by going to the eye doctor and have them opened. The ability to see in a new way is like being let out of prison, having your chains cut, throwing off a heavy load. Like Tyler Perry, it was only when I chose to "see my past in a new way" that I was no longer a victim of it.

We cannot do anything about our pasts, but we can choose whether we want to be victims of it. Once I began to understand that my Dad "did what he knew how," I was able to move from anger to compassion. I thank God that I was able to bury all that resentment, even before I buried him.

"Seeing in a new way" is exactly the conclusion Jesus came to in his search for clarity during his forty days in the desert. Coming out of the desert, he began to preach "conversion." *Metanoiete* means "change the way you see." Change the way you look at things and heaven will open up to you. Once things change in you, things around you will look very different." The devil tried to get Jesus to change things. Jesus resisted that temptation. Instead, Jesus called for an internal change within people, believing that if people would change inside, things outside them would also change. A new life begins with having your eyes opened.

In John's Gospel reading we have a wonderful story about a bunch of blind people: one who **can't** see and others who **won't** see. All of them need Jesus in order to be able to "see." In this story, Jesus uses the occasion of healing physical blindness to tell us something about the healing of spiritual blindness.

The man born blind, not only regains his physical sight, but step-by-step he begins to see Jesus in a new way. At first, he says he tells people he doesn't know who this Jesus is who healed him. As the story unfolds, he calls Jesus a "prophet" and finally "Lord."

The Pharisees and his parents can see physically, but they are spiritually blind and refuse "to see in a new way." The Pharisees are blinded by their own rigid religious structures. They can't see the beauty of this great healing, a blind man getting his sight. All they can see is that this healing took place on the Sabbath day and healing was illegal on the Sabbath day. The parents are blinded by their fear of being ostracized by neighbors, friends and organized religion if they admitted to this healing. They conveniently choose not to know and not to see. "Ask him," they say, "he is old enough to speak for himself." Both Pharisees and parents are afraid of "seeing in a new way" because it would mean their cozy little routines would be disrupted. It was convenient for them not to see and so remain stuck in their chosen blindness.

I am amazed when I talk to "stuck" people. I believe that most people who are stuck are basically people who are blinded by their inability to "see in a new way." They whine and cry and wait to be rescued, but they cannot change their minds and look at their situations from a new angle. They can't "let go" of their old way of thinking and seeing, and so remain stuck in their blindness. They are like the monkeys I read about several years ago. To catch these monkeys for the zoo, people would cut a hole in a tree, just small enough for a monkey to stick his hand into. Then they fill it with peanuts. When the monkey sticks his hand into the hole and grabs the peanuts he cannot pull his hand back out. Instead of letting go of the peanuts, they howl and cry till someone comes and hauls them off to the zoo. All they had to do was to let go of the peanuts. People are a lot like that: they cannot let go of the way they see things and so remain trapped, whining and crying all the while.

Some people simply cannot "let go" of the way they see things. They clutch at beliefs like: life ought to be fair, parents ought to be perfect, spouses should not let each other down, the church ought to be perfect, things ought to make sense and people ought to respect you, love you and meet your needs. And, of course, when life isn't fair, when parents and churches aren't perfect, when spouses let them down, when things don't make sense and when people do not meet their needs, they fall apart and remain stuck in their belief that if they just don't like it enough, it will go away. All they would have to do to free themselves is to "let go" of their old beliefs and "see things in a new way."

Jesus was right, "If you were physically blind, there is no sin in that, but when you choose to be blind, your sin remains, you keep your own suffering going." Tyler Perry is right, too, when he says, "My life changed once things changed in me."

What about you? What **situations** do you need to "look at" in a new way? What **people** do you need to "look at" in a new way? Is the way you have been "looking at" these situations and people still causing you pain? If so, ask God for healing. Ask God for a new set of eyes. Once things change *in* you, life will change for the better *for* you.

FIFTH, WE ARE INVITED TO THE GRAVE

*"Did I not tell you that if you believe you will
see the glory of God?"*
John 11:40

Jesus had a large circle of friends, both men and women. On the fifth Sunday of Lent, we get an inside glimpse at three of those friends: Martha, her sister Mary and their brother Lazarus from the little town of Bethany on the outskirts of Jerusalem. It was that special place in the life of Jesus where he and his disciples could stop in, get some rest, enjoy a hot meal and then go on their way. If you pay attention to the details of John's gospel story about Martha, Mary and Lazarus, you soon realize just how close Jesus was to these people. This is a story about intimate friends, affectionate friends.

First, we know that this Mary was the Mary who kissed Jesus' feet in public, washing them with her tears, drying them with her hair, and rubbing them with perfumed oil. (When was the last time anybody kissed your feet? You must be pretty close to do that, not to mention in public!) Read down the text and you see that John underlines, again and again, just how intimate these people were with Jesus: "Lord, the one you love is sick." "Jesus loved

Martha and her sister and Lazarus very much." "See how much he loved him!" They are even so close that these two women can "chew him out" and get away with it: "Lord, if you had been here, my brother would never have died." And finally, seeing Mary weep, we are told that "Jesus began to weep," too.

One usually thinks of this story as the "raising of Lazarus," but Jesus' raising of Lazarus actually occupies a very small part of this story. Of the forty-four verses that constitute this story, only seven of them take place at Lazarus' tomb. The miracle of the raising of Lazarus is the climax of this story; it is not the center. This is a dialogue between Jesus and the two women about God's power in our lives.

In his gospel, John's stories always have two levels: one on the surface which is true and another below the surface which is truer still. This intimate story is meant to reveal to us not only the depth of **their** friendship, but also how intimate is God's relationship with **us**. The pain of this family is the pain of God for his people. By listening in to the dialogue, we are also taught what they were taught: about the depth of God's love for us, about God's willingness to give us new life, and about God's power over our worst enemy – death.

(1) We are taught about the depths of God's love for us. One of the biggest challenges I have faced as a priest is to convince people of God's unconditional love for

them. Why is it that so many of us have been trained by people who have dismissed these intimate stories of God's love and have combed through the Scriptures, piecing together condemning, judging, and damning messages that they turn into a religion? Why did they, and why do we, find those negative messages more believable? I have received more letters questioning my "too lenient notions of God's love" than any other critical letters since I became a priest. Jesus revealed the "true God," not this "false mean god" that people have created since Adam and Eve. Even in that story, God says to Adam and Eve, "Who told you that you were naked?" (Genesis 3:11). In other words, "Who told you that you were bad, separated from me, and defective? I certainly didn't!" Jesus came to talk us out of the mean God we keep creating in our own minds. I can't imagine trying to live my religion without being in love with God. I can't imagine practicing a religion based on fear and dread.

(2) By listening in on the conversation between Jesus, Martha and Mary, we are taught also about God's willingness to give us new life. This eternal life is on both sides of death. Death does not have the last word. Eternal life is not just some promise for the future; it is available to us right now. We are in it, as we speak! Through Jesus and in Jesus, those of us who are "dead on our feet" can be resurrected now. We can be born again. We can act boldly on our own behalf to live purposeful lives, to help others,

and to claim the powers that lie dormant within us. One of my favorite old movies is *Harold and Maude*. This is Maude's message to Harold throughout the movie: "Oh, how the world dearly loves a cage! There are a lot of people who enjoy being dead." Jesus came, not just to bring a wonderful life after we are dead, but right now!

(3) And, as this gospel teaches us, God has power over our worst enemy – death. We live in a death-denying culture. Some of our expensive funeral practices would leave outsiders with the impression that we believe that we are going to come up with a cure for death someday. That makes about as much sense as leaving the runway lights on for Amelia Earhart. We don't even know how to die. Modern medical technology robs us of the spiritual experience of "letting go" of this part of our life. Through Jesus and in Jesus, we are able to see in death that "life is changed, not ended." I feel sorry for those who are conscious at death's door without this faith.

Over the years, I have had the awesome privilege of talking to some very conscious people getting ready to die: especially those with AIDS and with cancer. Some were not pious people, but most were deeply spiritual. Some were able to tell me that they accepted their approaching deaths and they wanted to "do it well." Some were extremely thankful for the "eternal life" they had experienced in this world. Some looked with "joyful hope" for the "eternal life" ahead of them. You know, if you're facing death, it doesn't get any better than that! I hope I can do half as well. I pray for the ability to be conscious, filled with gratitude and ready to go when the time comes. Yes, I want to be conscious. I want to choose to let go and leap into that great unknown, to leap into the arms of God.

The message in this gospel is this: God loves you very, very much. He wants you to enjoy the eternal life that you experience right now, and he wants you to know that death does not have the last word. You can enjoy "eternal life" forever, yes starting right now.

CONCLUSION

I hope you have enjoyed our journey through the hotspots of Lent: the desert, the mountain, the well, the doctor and the grave. The disciplines of Lent – prayer fasting and almsgiving – are important *external* ascetical practices, but it is what happen *inside* us that count. Unless there is some change in our hearts, minds, outlooks and behaviors, all those ascetical practices are, in my book, just one big waste of time. As I Samuel (16:7) says, "People see externals, but God sees into the heart."

Hopefully, at the end of Lent, we are better people, people with an improved vision and a better perspective on who we are and what matters to us the most. Hopefully we are a bit happier and more focused on the greater journey of life. Of course, this result is not something we can manufacture on our own, but only a gift that comes to us through our cooperation with God's help. In this regard, I have always found the words of William. H. Murray so very true and personally helpful on my own journey.

"Until one is committed, there is hesitancy, the chance to draw back. Concerning all acts of initiative (and creation), there is one elementary truth, the ignorance of which kills countless ideas and splendid plans: that the moment one definitely commits oneself, then Providence moves too. All sorts of things occur to help one that would never otherwise have occurred. A whole stream of events issues from the decision, raising in one's favor all manner of unforeseen incidents and meetings and material assistance, which no man could have dreamed would have come his way. Whatever you can do, or dream you can do, begin it. Boldness has genius, power, and magic in it. Begin it now."

www.ingramcontent.com/pod-product-compliance
Lightning Source LLC
Chambersburg PA
CBHW072038060426
42449CB00010BA/2325